Contents

Dictionary structure

Beginners – already new to the foreign language – may be baffled by the structure of bilingual dictionaries. It is therefore useful to let them 'play' with dictionaries so that they can learn to find their way round them.

Suggestions

Two halves

Do all students realise there are two halves to a bilingual dictionary? Do they know which is which? Do they know where the second half starts? If they don't, they may waste valuable time.

Say words, either in English or in the target language, and ask students merely to open their dictionaries to the half where they'll find that word. They can then practise this in pairs.

Make sure students can easily spot where the second half of their dictionary starts. If they can't, suggest they use something to mark the point.

Other sections

In most dictionaries, students will come across other sections in addition to the two bilingual halves: verb tables, list of abbreviations, etc. At beginner level, simply say a few words about those sections and advise students to ignore them at this early stage.

What's on a page?

The page structure may not be readily understood by weaker students. Ask students to work out:

- how many columns there are on a page
- what the words in bold/colour are (headwords)
- what the words at the very top of the page are for.

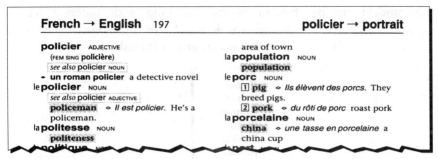

Collins Easy Learning French Dictionary

Students should also understand that, as in monolingual dictionaries, words are listed alphabetically.

Alphabetical order

One cannot assume expertise at looking up words that are listed alphabetically.

Train students to find the correct first letter. First practise using English words, then move on to foreign words. Students can then practise in pairs.

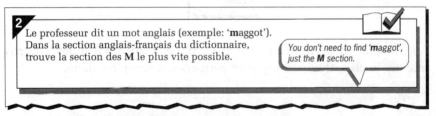

Developing Dictionary Skills in French

Familiarise students with the foreign alphabet.

Not all dictionaries are the same, but this sheet will help you find your way round the dictionary. It will also help you practise the alphabet.

Developing Dictionary Skills in German

Ask students to list foreign words beginning with different letters alphabetically. It is best to use words which are topic-related. Use first names, names of towns or words very similar to English.

Planet
Venus
Neptun
Pluto
Merkur
Jupiter
Uranus
Erde

Now practise this with words beginning with the same letter.

Países
Australia
China
Canarias
Albania
Canadá
Chile
Argentina
Corea

Ask students to devise their own tasks, using words from topics covered recently in class, then to swap with partners and complete them.

Building up speed

In class, at home or in exam conditions, slow dictionary use wastes time and affects performance and motivation. Besides, as with many other classroom activities, working against the clock can bring a welcome game dimension to the work.

Suggestions

Working against the clock

Give students a list of words to look up and ask them to time themselves and keep a record of their performance, or to race against their partners. Repeat the exercise at regular intervals to encourage students to improve their speed.

To make sure students do look up and find the words, ask them to write the translation down. It is therefore advisable to focus on very short dictionary entries.

avispero [aβis'pero] *nm* wasp's nest
avispón [aβis'pon] *nm* hornet

oruga [o'ruɣa] *nf* caterpillar
orzuelo [or'θwelo] *nm* (MED) stye

Collins Pocket Spanish Dictionary

Not just translation

To make the practice more appealing, do not just ask students to find and translate words: suggest a purpose beyond mere translation, such as, in this case, matching up animals with their preferred food.

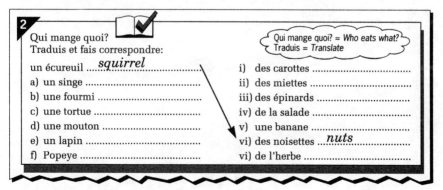

2

Qui mange quoi?
Traduis et fais correspondre:

un écureuil .....*squirrel*.....

a) un singe ....
b) une fourmi ....
c) une tortue ....
d) une mouton ....
e) un lapin ....
f) Popeye ....

Qui mange quoi? = Who eats what?
Traduis = Translate

i) des carottes ....
ii) des miettes ....
iii) des épinards ....
iv) de la salade ....
v) une banane ....
vi) des noisettes .....*nuts*.....
vi) de l'herbe ....

With brighter students, use short phrases as well as words and with older students who still need speed practice, use more mature topic areas and provide opportunities for stating opinions.

2

Problèmes d'adolescence
Traduis et classe les problèmes de 1 à 10.

1 = le plus grand problème

la famille .... ☐   les copains et copines .... ☐

la peau .... ☐   la croissance physique .... ☐

la mode .... ☐   le manque de liberté .... ☐

l'argent .... ☐   le prof de français .... ☐

le racisme .... ☐   un problème d'amour .... ☐

.... minutes   .... /10

Finding the correct entry

Awareness of alphabetical order is not always enough for finding the correct dictionary entry. There are a number of potential pitfalls students need to be made aware of.

Suggestions

Spelling matters

Alert students to the danger of looking up the wrong word through lack of concentration – or poor spelling skills! A teacher once reported how one of his students had allegedly eaten 'un élan au chocolat' (a chocolate moose. . .).

Students can ensure that they have looked up the correct entry if they are familiar with key abbreviations for parts of speech, and recognise the usefulness of words in brackets, the examples provided or cross-checking in the other half of the dictionary (time consuming!).

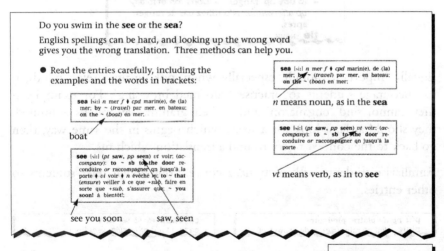

Alert pupils to near-identical foreign words which mean different things depending on accents:

Spanish
solo or sólo?
como or cómo?

Browsing

In the main, one is unlikely to find conjugated verbs or feminine plural adjectives listed as separate entries.

Make students aware of this, and use this as a tool for explaining that having a dictionary is no replacement for lexical and grammatical awareness.

This may also need to be spelt out to students when looking up English words. For example, students should look up 'sneeze' rather than 'sneezing'. In some dictionaries, verbs in English are preceded by 'to', so you can identify them at a glance.

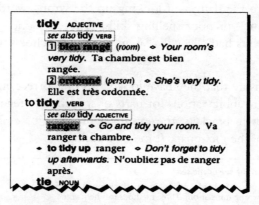

Equally important though, especially when looking up foreign words, is to encourage students to practise 'informed browsing'. For example, if they cannot find 'engañaron' and if their grammar awareness is limited, they should at least look for a word which begins in the same way, then go back to the context to try to find a translation which fits.

Familiarise students with dictionary conventions which refer students to other entries.

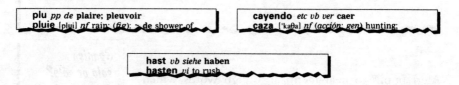

Multi-purpose entries

'It's not in here!' is a common reaction when students make the mistake of assuming that each and every word is listed as a separate entry.

Develop students' awareness of word families and show that, in many dictionaries, several words from the same family may be listed under the same entry.

Garten ['gartən] (-s, ⁺) *m* garden; ~**arbeit** *f* gardening; ~**gerät** *nt* gardening tool; ~**lokal** *nt* beer garden; ~**schere** *f* pruning shears *pl*; ~**tür** *f* garden gate
Gärtner(in) ['gɛrtnər(ın)] (-s, -) *m(f)*

3 Vervollständige diese Tabelle

Wort	Bedeutung
Glück	luck, fortune
glückern	to succeed
a) gluckern	....
b) Glückskind	....
c) Glückspiel	....

Developing Dictionary Skills in German

To practise this, ask students to find as many words as they can under one headword.

Explain that this may also apply to short phrases, and explain the meaning of the symbol ~ as used in dictionary entries, either in relation to compound words or short phrases. Incidentally, phrases such as 'wet suit' are generally translated under the first word ('wet'), regardless of the parts of speech of each word.

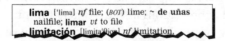

lima ['lima] *nf* file; (*BOT*) lime; ~ **de uñas** nailfile; **limar** *vt* to file
limitación [limita'θjon] *nf* limitation.

Point out that hyphenated words, such as 'bloc-notes', are often – although not always – listed separately from the entries for each constituent word.

hang-gliding ['hæŋɡlaɪdıŋ] *n* Drachenfliegen *nt*
hangover ['hæŋəʊvə] *n* Kater *m*

hang: ~-gliding ['hæŋɡlaɪdıŋ] *n* deltaplane *m*, vol *m* libre; ~over ['hæŋəʊvə] *n* (*after drinking*) gueule *f* de bois; ~-up ['hæŋʌp] *n* complexe *m*
hanker ['hæŋkə] *vi:* **to ~ after** avoir en-

Demystifying dictionary entries

A specific dictionary entry can be even more baffling than dictionary structure as a whole: words in colour or in black and white, different types of brackets, different fonts, abbreviations, words in bold, symbols, odd signs... Only very bright students stand a chance of working out their significance on their own.

Suggestions

Start with short entries as a means of familiarising students with standard abbreviations.

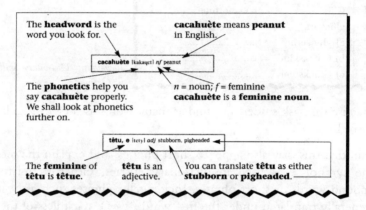

Do not neglect to look at English entries. In the entries below, notice how the position of the abbreviations *m* and *f* differs from the foreign language entries, where they come *before* the English translation of the noun.

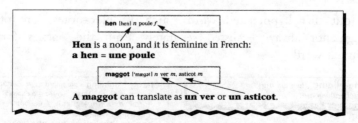

Decide on how many – or how few – abbreviations students need to understand to get by. For many students in the early years, this may be little more than:

> **m or nm**
> **f or nf**
> **nt (German)**
> **sg**
> **pl**
> **adj**
> **vb/vi/vr/vt (the v is all that matters to a number of students)**

At a higher level and when looking at longer entries, the use of diamonds, to point out different parts of speech, or numbers, when there are many translations for the one word, may need explaining.

mould [məʊld] (*US* **mold**) *n* Form *f*; (*mildew*) Schimmel *m* ♦ *vt* (*also fig*) formen; **~er** *vi* (*decay*) vermodern; **~y** *adj* schimmelig
moult [məʊlt] (*US* **molt**) *vi* sich mausern

KEYWORD

at [æt] *prep* **1** (*referring to position*) en; (*direction*) a; ~ **the top** en lo alto; ~ **home/school** en casa/la escuela; **to look** ~ **sth/sb** mirar algo/a uno
2 (*referring to time*): ~ **4 o'clock** a las 4; ~ **night** por la noche; ~ **Christmas** en Navidad; ~ **times** a veces
3 (*referring to rates, speed etc*): ~ **£1 a kilo** a una libra el kilo; **two** ~ **a time** de

Selecting the correct translation

This section focuses largely on what students tend to be seeking when using a bilingual dictionary: a translation! It also shows what else dictionaries can help with (checking gender, for instance). Here again, the task is not always as straightforward as it sounds, hence the need to make dictionary practice activities as appealing as any other language work.

Suggestions

Use of abbreviations

For translation from English, students need to understand gender abbreviations to decide on which article to use. For translation into English, they need to understand that some words have several meanings depending on gender, for example:

> *der Kunde = customer* *die Kunde = news*
> *der Leiter = leader* *die Leiter = ladder*
> *der Hut = hat* *die Hut = care*

Students also need to know that some words have different meanings depending on whether they are singular or plural.

> *esposa = wife*
> *esposas = handcuffs*

Some words translate differently depending on parts of speech.

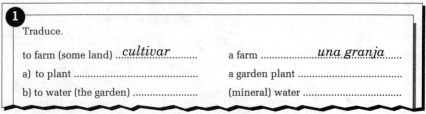

> **1**
> Traduce.
>
> to farm (some land) ...*cultivar*......   a farm ....*una granja*......
>
> a) to plant ....   a garden plant ....
>
> b) to water (the garden) ....   (mineral) water ....

Developing Dictionary Skills in Spanish

Other clues for translation from English

When several translations are offered for the same English word, train students to look at the words in brackets, any examples given, the context and – only if all else fails – to cross-check in the other half of the dictionary.

Other clues for translation into English

When the dictionary offers several English translations for a foreign word, again students need to look at the words in brackets or the context in order to select the correct one. The funnier the examples you use to alert students to the dangers of incorrect translation, the better:

> *Mon père est avocat.*   *Is dad really an avocado?*
> *Estos canapés son deliciosos.*   *What's for dinner? A sofa?*
> *Seine Augen sind blau.*   *How did his eyes get drunk?*

Other pitfalls

Some students are put off by the fact that a translation may be made up of a different number of words from the original. Practice that includes examples they have come across – be it unconsciously – in the past can reassure them. Remind them that languages do not mirror each other exactly. They need to recognise occasions when words may not translate in the same order or into the same number of words, for example:

> *a maths room = une salle de maths*
> *I agree = estoy de acuerdo*

Students' attempts to translate idioms into the foreign language should set alarm bells ringing. When a phrase does not mean what the sum total of its individual components means, there may be trouble ahead. If a herring is 'un maquereau', is a red herring 'un maquereau rouge'?

Unless they have access to more comprehensive dictionaries, students are best advised to avoid using such phrases.

Verbs

When it comes to translating verbs, the dictionary cannot replace grammar competence. Students should therefore rely as much as they can on what they have learnt and practised in class and as little as possible on the dictionary.

To ease translation, train students to look at the subject of the verb as well as the verb itself, especially those students who have difficulty in recognising verb endings.

For translation into the target language, teach more able students to distinguish between *vt* and *vi*. For translation into English, the context often makes the need to understand *vr* unnecessary.

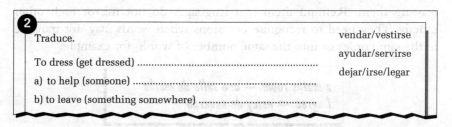

2

Traduce.   vendar/vestirse

                                                                      ayudar/servirse
To dress (get dressed) ....
                                                                      dejar/irse/legar
a) to help (someone) ....

b) to leave (something somewhere) ....

What else is in the dictionary?

There may be a time when the additional information contained in a dictionary can be very useful.

Suggestions

Verb tables

Verbs tables are best tackled only with students who have a sufficient grasp of grammar to understand how they work. Practice using verb tables can help these students memorise verbs more easily.

Occasionally set straightforward exercises for learning tenses and moods where students can use verb tables if they wish to help them fill in a gapped table you have supplied, but impose a strict time limit, as a time challenge focuses the brain.

Phonetics

While not needing to learn the entire phonetical system, some students may find a degree of familiarity with phonetics useful:

- for learning to pronounce words where English pronunciation may interfere

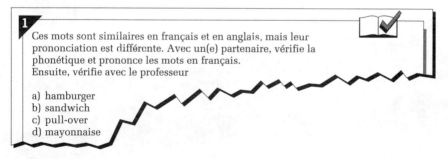

1

Ces mots sont similaires en français et en anglais, mais leur prononciation est différente. Avec un(e) partenaire, vérifie la phonétique et prononce les mots en français.
Ensuite, vérifie avec le professeur

a) hamburger
b) sandwich
c) pull-over
d) mayonnaise

- for finding out which letters in a word are silent
- when confronted with letters or combinations of letters that can represent several sounds, for example *bateau* and *dos*, *shampooing* and *chandelier*, *Danemark* and *chrétien*.

List of abbreviations

> **cane** [keɪn] n (*BOT*) Rohr nt; (*stick*) Stock
> m ♦ vt (*BRIT*: *SCH*) schlagen
> canine [ˈkeɪnaɪn]

In the above extract, *(BOT)* and *(BRIT: SCH)* can be of little use to students unless they know where to find out what they mean. Most dictionaries include a glossary of the abbreviations used.

Other information

Some pocket-size dictionaries also contain specific information about common lexical areas, such as numbers or time phrases. Regular reminders to students of what else they can find and when they can use the infomation may be useful.

Dictionary avoidance techniques

Suggestions

Cognates and near cognates

Students often believe that the only words they can possibly understand are those the teacher has taught them. They may not readily assume that foreign words which resemble English have the same meaning.

From an early stage, bring students into contact with a vast number of cognates, both in tasks focusing specifically on this issue and in other dictionary-related tasks (see the task on teenage problems on p8).

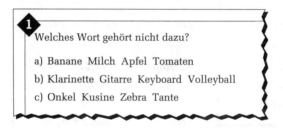

1 Welches Wort gehört nicht dazu?

a) Banane Milch Apfel Tomaten
b) Klarinette Gitarre Keyboard Volleyball
c) Onkel Kusine Zebra Tante

Do the same with near cognates. Here, the increased level of difficulty also means a greater feeling of achievement for students.

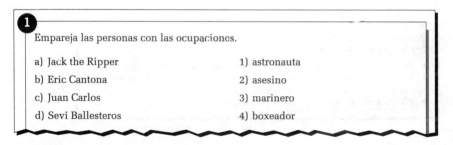

1 Empareja las personas con las ocupaciones.

a) Jack the Ripper	1) astronauta
b) Eric Cantona	2) asesino
c) Juan Carlos	3) marinero
d) Sevi Ballesteros	4) boxeador

Word formation

Make students as aware as possible of parallels between languages to facilitate understanding of the foreign language. Although this is not a foolproof technique, it can help students make informed guesses to produce language when time is short. However, for this to be of any use, students need to be aware of the lexical areas where this tends to apply most often (jobs, personality).

Spanish	
biology	*biología*
religious	*religioso*

French	
actor	*acteur*
musician	*musicien*

Familiarise students with beginnings and endings (prefixes and suffixes).

faire/refaire/défaire
envoyer/renvoyer
discret/indiscret

Ending	*Effect*
-chen	*small/little*
-in	*female*
-heit	*makes a noun*

To facilitate language production, familiarise students with any other helpful patterns.

You can find out the gender of a word without using the dictionary. Try learning these patterns:
- Words ending in -ich, -ig, -ing, and -ling are masculine (der).
- Words ending in -n, -ei, -heit, -keit, -schaft, -ung are feminine (die). Most words ending in -e are feminine.
- Words ending in -chen, -lein, -nis and -tum are neuter (das).

Work based on awareness of word families is an aid to understanding – and, possibly, production – of unknown words. Awareness of context should be emphasised at the same time.

2   Lis cette liste et traduis les mots **en caractères gras** (a–g) sans dictionnaire.

construire (to build)   manger (to eat)   chaud (hot)   la mode (fashion)
traduire (to translate)   casser (to break)   envoyer (to send)   congeler (to freeze)

reconstruire une maison .....*to rebuild*...

a) un texte **intraduisible** ....

b) un verre **incassable** ....

c) **renvoyer** une lettre ....

Other clues to understanding

All reading skills can – and should – contribute to minimising dictionary use. When teaching reading skills, always present them explicitly as serving this purpose.

Encourage students to read the rubric and the task – if applicable – before the text itself. Also encourage students to start from what they understand (e.g. key words) and to look for any other clues to understanding (e.g. layout, visual clues).

If students are reluctant to believe the message about looking for key words first, try an experiment. Show them a text from which you have removed just about everything except for key words and ask them if they can work out the overall meaning of what you are showing them. If the language is suited to the ability level of the students, they will most likely say yes. Then show them the whole text, which is likely to contain some difficult but superfluous language which might have put them off, had they seen the entire passage from the outset. This method can be used with near beginners or more advanced students.

(....) avance de tropas (...) carreteras a Banja Luka (....) coches, tractores (...) miles de civiles serbios (....) Muchos vehículos (....) abandonados (....) sin combustible.

Mientras prosigue el avance de tropas, las carreteras que van a Banja Luka se abarrotan de coches, tractores y carros, transportando a miles de civiles serbios que huyen de la ofensiva. Muchos vehículos han quedado abandonados en la cuneta sin combustible.

For recognition purposes − especially when reading − encourage students to look at the context or to use their awareness of parts of speech in order to deduce the meaning of individual words. Understanding the context is also useful for spotting 'false friends'.

¡Qué frío! Estoy constipado desde hace dos semanas.	*Ich gebe dir einen guten Rat.*	*Je peux mettre mes T-shirts dans la commode?*

Each language has its own range of characteristics which allow for the development of techniques that can aid a student's understanding through certain language-specific tricks. For example in German, when confronted with a long and complex-looking word, saying it out loud can often help.

Students sometimes appear to think that since what they are reading is 'foreign', common sense need no longer apply. This could not be further from the truth. Remind them to use common sense, logic and world knowledge as much as possible to solve comprehension problems.

Productive skills

When time only allows for minimal dictionary use, simplification (or even small white lies) can help overcome obstacles. When memory fails, saying that mum works in a supermarket, although less precise, is a suitable alternative to explaining that she is deputy assistant manager.

> **Miss, how do I say my dad is a guillotine operator?**

Some students, however bright, miss the chance of a top examination grade through lack of mental flexibility. They are forever trying to produce an exact translation of a perfect sentence thay have constructed in English. Flexibility requires training. The next best thing to sending them on a course on lateral thinking may be the type of exercise suggested below. This can also rekindle the motivation level of students tired of potentially unstimulating transactional work.

Es importante utilizar una diversidad de palabras y estructuras para sacar buenas notas en español. Sin embargo, a veces no es ni necesario ni práctico buscar palabras en el diccionario. Si no sabes cómo decir algo, puedes explicarlo de otro modo.

Empareja estas frases.

Frases difíciles

a) La variedad climática es muy fuerte.

b) Una serie de pueblos de muy diversa procedencia vinieron a instalarse en la Península Ibérica.

c) España approvecha un 50% de su superficie como tierra de cultivo.

Frases fáciles

1) La agricultura utiliza el 50% de la tierra española.

2) El clima puede cambiar mucho.

3) Hoy la pesca no es tan importante para la economía porque hay menos pescado.

Flexibility, combined with the ability to recycle language first encountered in a different context, can also help overcome obstacles generated by prepositions and phrasal verbs. Encourage students to build up their own records of all the various ways they have come across of translating key prepositions. Ask them to learn examples by heart. With regards to phrasal verbs, wherever possible encourage students to think simple. There is very often an English equivalent which is easier to translate, for example:

to make up = to invent (inventer)
to hang on = to wait (attendre)
to turn up = to arrive (arriver)

Dictionary use in the exam

Students who believe that the dictionary will solve all their problems in the exam run the risk of overusing it and failing to complete the tasks set. Many will need advice.

Golden rules

For each exam paper, check that you know under what conditions dictionary use is allowed.

Do everything you can do without the dictionary first.

Rehearse ways of minimising dictionary use.

Make sure your dictionary is suited to your needs.

Make sure you know what is where.

Rehearse how to avoid looking up the wrong words.

Rehearse ways of selecting the correct translation.

Practise using your dictionary under exam conditions in class and at home.

Listening

If dictionary use is allowed by your exam board, it will only be for a small part of the listening exam.

Pre-listening:
- first look at the examples given before each task to work out what to do. You may not need to read the rubrics
- then if you have time, look at the task content and check one or two words which seem essential, for example if you see a picture of a shower and cannot remember the word for 'shower'.

Post-listening:
- look up words whose sounds you recognised but whose meaning you cannot remember
- do not attempt to look up totally unfamiliar words which you do not even know how to spell.

Speaking

- in your preparation time, read all the tasks first
- avoid using your dictionary for what you should have prepared prior to the exam
- think simple to minimise dictionary use. Use the exam to show off what you can do rather than to make up for what you cannot
- use your dictionary for looking up individual words rather than structures
- only look up what seems essential, like a key word for a roleplay
- check whether you can take notes into the exam room. If not, you will have to memorise the words you look up.

Reading

Obviously, here again, dictionary use needs to be kept to a minimum. Students should read through the paper first, studying the rubrics and looking for key words. If they come across a word that they feel may be important but do not understand, they should underline it and see how far they get before they have to look it up.

Writing

> How long is the written exam?
>
> Plan your time carefully.
>
> j) Allow time to .... your work when you have finished.
>
> k) Three of the rules for speaking (a–i above) apply just as much to writing. Which three are they?
>
> l) If you don't know a word or can't find it, don't .... Write something slightly ....

Just like students who write a plan after writing an essay, simply to keep the teacher happy, students may be tempted to ignore advice about limiting dictionary use. When doing a piece of writing in class or at home, they should keep a record of the words they look up, so that you can discuss them if necessary. Also they must never forget how long it takes to look up ten words!

Dictionary work with a smile

Students soon switch off if dictionary work is not adapted to their needs or consists of little more than a diet of 'translate this, translate that'. Here are a few suggestions to ensure success and enjoyment.

Build up dictionary skills progressively, and recycle them regularly within new topic areas.

Do not try to teach everything there is to know about a dictionary. Set priorities in the light of syllabuses and students' needs.

Address the issue of the use of the target language or English just as you do in other areas of your work. Where explanations in English are needed, minimise them by giving clear examples. Set tasks in the target language. Use pictures to minimise the need for English words in some of the tasks.

Frequently set students targets such as working against the clock or looking up no more than a specified number of words.

Make the tasks varied and attractive:

- disguise the mere 'looking-up-and-translating' process by giving an ulterior purpose to the tasks (games, stating preferences, general knowledge, matching up with artwork etc.)
- whenever possible, organise the work round a topic area rather than random words
- provide opportunities for dealing with unfamiliar language by tackling familiar topics more in depth (looking up more pets, more jobs, etc) and by exploring topic areas beyond your usual schemes of work (general knowledge, current news, etc.).

Facilitate a more autonomous approach:

- use tasks that can be carried out over a period of time on a self-access basis according to needs (for classroom, cover lessons or homework use)
- wherever possible, give easy access to answers
- provide opportunities for extension work (ask students to make up tasks of their own after carrying out the tasks set by you).

Conclusion

As a conclusion, one cannot emphasise certain key messages too much, especially to those students who believe that having a dictionary can replace any effort on their part.

> *Using a dictionary takes up valuable time.*
> *A language is not just a collection of words.*
> *Having a dictionary should not replace learning by heart.*
> *Grammar awareness makes dictionary use easier.*
> *Poor dictionary use is worse than no dictionary use.*

Collins Tips for Busy Language Teachers

Effective Use of a Bilingual Dictionary at 11–16

If you would like to inspect any of the other titles in this series or other resources mentioned in this book, please **tick the relevant boxes, fill in your details overleaf, photocopy or cut out this form and return** to:

HarperCollins Publishers
Modern Languages/Collins Educational
FREEPOST
London W6 8BR

Title	ISBN	Price	Approval/ Inspection Copy	Order Qty
Mixed Pack (1 copy of each)	0 00 320239 9	£11.70	☐	_____
Motivating Reluctant Learners at 14–16	0 00 320226 7	£2.25		_____
Stretching the More Able at 14–16	0 00 320227 5	£2.25		_____
Brightening up Transactional Topics at 14–16	0 00 320228 3	£2.25		_____
Independent Reading – how to make it work	0 00 320229 1	£2.25		_____
Homework and Cover Lessons – handy tips	0 00 320231 3	£2.25		_____
Developing Dictionary Skills in French	0 00 320194 5	£26.50	☐	_____
Developing Dictionary Skills in Spanish	0 00 320233 X	£26.50	☐	_____
Developing Dictionary Skills in German	0 00 320232 1	£26.50	☐	_____
Collins Pocket French Dictionary	0 00 470396 0	£6.99	☐	_____
Collins Pocket German Dictionary	0 00 470397 9	£6.99	☐	_____
Collins Pocket Spanish Dictionary	0 00 470398 7	£6.99	☐	_____
Collins Easy Learning French Dictionary	0 00 470714 1	£5.99	☐	_____
Collins Easy Learning German Dictionary (May 97)	0 00 470712 5	£5.99	☐	_____
Collins Easy Learning Spanish Dictionary (May 98)	0 00 470933 0	£5.99	☐	_____
Modern Languages Catalogue	0 58 380108 0	FREE		_____

We are always looking to expand the *Collins Tips for Busy Language Teachers* series and would be interested to know what topics you would like to see covered in the future. (Please tick the boxes below or add your own suggestions.)

☐ Post–16: bridging the gap

☐ Making Grammar Practice at 14–16 More Fun

☐ Languages for Special Needs Students at 14–16

☐ Testing in the Target Language

☐ Other _____

Mr/Ms/Miss/Mrs: _____

Position: _____

School: _____

Address: _____

_____

_____

Postcode: _____

LEA: _____

E-mail address: _____